A Door to Secrets

Riddles in Rhyme

Tony Mitton

Illustrated by David Parkins

CAMBRIDGE
UNIVERSITY PRESS

Cambridge Reading

General Editors
Richard Brown and Kate Ruttle

Consultant Editor
Jean Glasberg

PUBLISHED BY THE PRESS SYNDICATE OF THE UNIVERSITY OF CAMBRIDGE
The Pitt Building, Trumpington Street, Cambridge CB2 1RP, United Kingdom

CAMBRIDGE UNIVERSITY PRESS
The Edinburgh Building, Cambridge CB2 2RU, United Kingdom
40 West 20th Street, New York, NY 10011-4211, USA
10 Stamford Road, Oakleigh, Melbourne 3166, Australia

Text © Tony Mitton 1998
Illustrations © David Parkins 1998

First published 1998
Reprinted 1998

Printed in the United Kingdom at the University Press, Cambridge

Typeset in Concorde

A catalogue record for this book is available from the British Library

ISBN 0 521 49841 4 paperback

CONTENTS

Haunted House

1

What's that whisper?
What's that cr*eeee*k?
What's that chill
upon my cheek?

What's that prickling
in my hair?
Who's that standing
on the stair?

CREEEEK!

2

Rattle, rattle,
clack, clack, clack.
Look right through me,
front to back.

I don't make wails
I don't make moans.
I just rattle.
I'm just bones.

5

3

Down in the kitchen
there's a funny smell.
Plop, fizz, bubble.
Is it a spell?

Yes, it'll make you
sneeze and itch.
But who is the cook?
It must be a . . .

4

Who's this man
in the long, black cape,
upside-down
in a bat-like shape?

Wait till sunset,
wait till night.
What big teeth!
They'll give you a fright.

Jungle

1

Up in a tree
you might see me.

Or down on the ground
I might be found,

sliding along
with a hissing sound.

8

2

I'm like a log
adrift on the river.
But give me a jog
and I'll make you shiver.

If you come by,
I'll open an eye.
And you'll think
that I'm taking a nap . . . SNAP!

3

I jump about.
I scream and shout.
I chatter and grin.
I scratch my skin.

I leap around
from tree to tree.
I'm a bit like you
but you can't catch me!

4

Hear me snarl.
Hear me growl.
See me sneaking.
Watch me prowl.

What's the pattern
on my back?
Yellow-brown
with spots of black.

Arabian Nights

1

Unroll me.
Get a surprise.
See how I float.
See how I rise.

Get ready.
Sit tight.
I'll fly you across
an Arabian night.

2

Dry, dry land.
Lots and lots and lots
of sand.

No water to drink.
No food to eat.

Just sand and sun
and blazing heat.

3

Magic bloke.
Made of smoke.

Brings you anything.
What's your wish?
Good luck? Treasure?
Food on a dish?

Want anything?
Rub this ring.

4

In the middle of the desert there's water.
In the middle of the desert there are trees.
In the middle of the desert there's soft, green shade
and a welcome, cooling breeze.
Now, let me see, I think that this
is what we call an . . .

SPACE

1

I fly like an arrow
with a tail of fire,
higher, higher,
fast and far,
to a distant planet
or a shining star.

2

I go boldly
into space
with a breathing bubble
over my face,
riding a rocket
to land on the moon.
Here I go!
See you soon . . .

17

1

Who sits and sings
upon the rocks?
Who combs her long
and golden locks?
Who has the power
to grant a wish?
Half-woman.
Half-fish.

2

Once I went
to far-off lands
with swelling belly
and many hands.
Now there's no-one
on my deck.
I'm a rotting
sunken . . .

3

I come quietly
gliding near,
bringing danger,
bringing fear.
When you see
my shape about,
take care,
watch out!

4

Inside my shell I'm shiny.
Inside my shell I'm round.
Sometimes I'm strung on a necklace,
but under the ocean I'm found.

fairytale Forest

1

What a funny cottage!
What a strange house!
A feast for a girl
or a boy or a mouse.

Is it a trick?
Or is it a treat?
This home looks like
something to eat.

2

Cheeks like a cherry,
red and ripe,
I sit on a toadstool
smoking a pipe.

Sneak up behind me.
Catch me if you can.
You won't find it easy,
I'm a clever little man.

23

3

Waiting, waiting,
deep in the wood,
for a plump little pig
or a girl with a hood.

What big eyes
and what sharp claws!
What big teeth!
What hungry jaws!

4

A nosy little girl
with golden hair
has eaten the porridge
and broken a chair.

And now that she's tired
and warm and fed,
she's fallen asleep
on a sweet, soft bed.

25

Underground Cavern

1

Shhh! I'm asleep.
Time to tiptoe.
Time to creep.
For if I wake
the ground will shake
and I'll breathe out flame.
Can you guess my name?

2

I'm upside-down
with my eyes shut tight
and I won't wake up
till the middle of the night.
Then I'll flit about fast
with my radar sight.
Did you guess me right?

3

Digging, digging,
deep in the mine,
down where the dazzling
diamonds shine.

A pretty princess
makes our tea.
Can you tell us:
who are we?

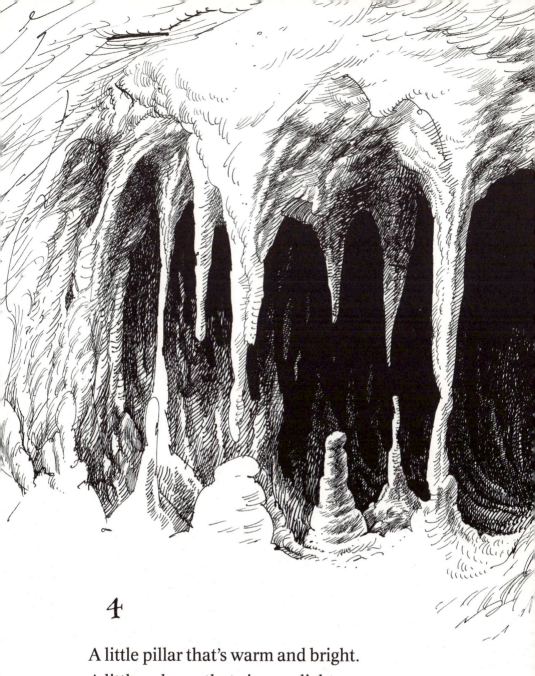

4

A little pillar that's warm and bright.
A little column that gives us light.
It grows a head of flickering flame.
Can you see now? What's its name?

Romance Castle

1

Hear my boots (clump, clump).
Hear my fist (thump, thump).
When I'm about (shiver, shiver)
the castle quakes (quiver, quiver).
When I shout (shiver, shiver)
the castle shakes (quiver, quiver).

2

Nobody sent me an invitation.
Nobody set me a place.
That's why I'm boiling with anger
and I'm wearing a frown on my face.
All of the others brought blessings
to lay on the baby's head.
But I am the one that they all forgot,
so I brought a curse instead!

Pirate Island

1

I am a place to hide away,
a place where pirates come to stay,
a little piece of sunny land
with coconut trees and golden sand.

2

Dark around,
in the middle clear,
I bring far-away things
near.
Good for looking
a very long way.
What am I?
Can you say?

Concrete Jungle

1

My name
is a bird's name.
Yes. The very same.

Towering high
above the town,
I can help things grow
or knock them down.

2

Many sounds
and many sights,
people, traffic,
flashing lights.

I am the way
for wheels and feet.
I am the place
you call the . . .

3

Lollipop colours
on a long, black stick.
Nice to look at,
but not to lick.

Nobody eats
this lollipop.
But when it turns red
they have to stop.

4

I rumble along
with a grumbly song
and lots of people inside.

I can carry you down
to the end of the town.
Jump on. I'll give you a ride.

Toymaker's Woodwork Shop

1

Bang! Bang! Bang!
What a noise!
What a din!
I use my head
to knock things in.

2

Round and round
on a twisty thread.
I'll make a hole
if you turn my head.

3

To and fro.
To and fro.
That's the way
I have to go.
Without your arm
I'll do no harm.
But my sharp teeth
are good
at cutting wood.

Factory

1

No beginning
and no end,
on I go
then round I bend.
Always carrying things along,
softly humming my rolling song.

2

Down to the bottom.
Up to the top.
Every now and then
I stop.
Wait for my doors
to open wide –
(see them slide) –
then step inside.

Wizard's Workshop

1

I spit and crackle
and give off heat.
Wood is what
I like to eat.
I'm fast and flickery,
swift and high,
but I settle to sleep
with a hiss
and a sigh.
What am I?

44

2

Hot and bubbly,
cool and still,
always ready
to slip and spill.
Use me carefully,
use me well,
and I'll help you simmer
a magic spell!

3

A door to secrets
that I can tell.
A box of words
with many a spell.

Come, see what's hid
under my lid.
Open and look,
I'm a . . .

4

I may seem just
a simple stick,
but watch out
or I'll swirl and flick.

I'll turn you into
a frog or a flower.
I am a stick
with special power.

ANSWERS

Haunted House
ghost
skeleton
witch
vampire

Jungle
snake
crocodile
monkey
leopard

Arabian Nights
magic carpet
desert
genie
oasis

Space
rocket
astronaut

Marine World
mermaid
wreck
shark
pearl

Fairytale Forest
gingerbread house
gnome
wolf
Goldilocks

Underground Cavern
dragon
bat
seven dwarfs
candle

Romance Castle
giant
wicked fairy
suit of armour
spinning wheel

Pirate Island
desert island
telescope

Concrete Jungle
crane
street
traffic lights
bus

Toymaker's Workshop
hammer
screw
saw

Factory
conveyor belt
lift

Wizard's Workshop
fire
water
book (of spells)
magic wand